In His Hands

The Continuing Adventures of

What Would Jesus Do?

Retold from Charles M. Sheldon's classic *In His Steps*

BY MACK THOMAS

·

ILLUSTRATIONS BY 'MAGINATION

Like the award-winning *What Would Jesus Do?*, this sequel is a special retelling for children of Charles M. Sheldon's immortal *In His Steps*, the all-time best-selling Christian novel. The final portion of that work—in which the scene shifts from a small Midwestern city to the clashing worlds of rich and poor in Chicago in the 1890s—provides the inspiration for this book, *In His Hands.*

IN HIS HANDS
published by Gold'n'Honey Books
a part of the Questar publishing family

© 1993 by Questar Publishers, Inc.

International Standard Book Number: 0-945564-44-9

Printed in the United States of America

For information:
QUESTAR PUBLISHERS, INC.
POST OFFICE BOX 1720
SISTERS, OREGON 97759

93 94 95 96 97 98 99 00 01 — 10 9 8 7 6 5 4 3 2 1

1

WINNING
BIG

Hooray, hooray!
Today was the day
for the Valley Fair.

And nearly everyone was there!

In the morning,
Bill was at the L & R Railroad booth.
A man in a blue uniform reached into
a ribbon-covered box—
and pulled out Bill's name!
And what was Bill's prize?
Free tickets for a train ride
to Chicago and back—for *four people!*

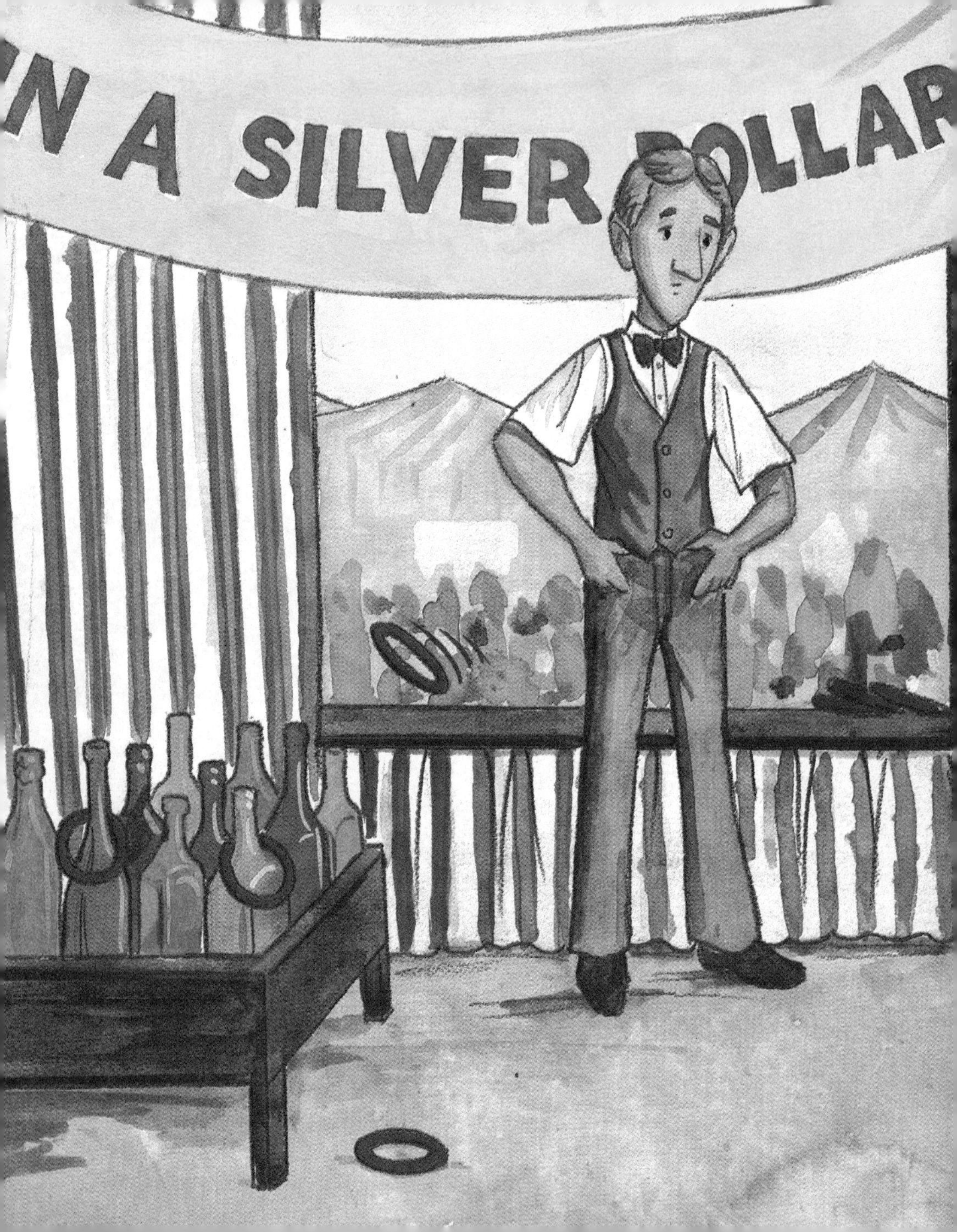
N A SILVER

And what's more, that afternoon Bill won
three silver dollars on the bottle ring toss.
Not even the bigger boys had done that well.

"What should I do with the money?"
Bill asked his friends Jack and Claire.
Together they repeated four wonderful words
they all had learned to say, every day:
What would Jesus do?

They decided to go and ask
their good friend Mister Manning.

In his fingers, the old blind man could feel
the smooth coins as Bill explained:
"I'd be happy to give the money to poor people,
to help them know how much God loves them.

"But I'd *also* like to save it for when I'm older...
but then I'd ALSO like to buy
something fun in Chicago.

"Mister Manning, what do you think Jesus would do?"

With a smile Mister Manning answered,
"I think He might do all three!
A dollar to give for God, a dollar to save,
and a dollar to spend in Chicago."

Bill quickly agreed to this wise plan.
Now he would have a whole silver dollar to spend,
plus a whole big city to spend it in.

What's more, he'd have good company.
For on this, his first-ever train ride,
his three best friends would go along.
And who were they?

Mister Manning, who had lived in Chicago
and said he had more work to do there;

Jack, who was born in Chicago
but had never been back;

And *Claire,* whose cousin Felicia lived there
in a big purple mansion.

Claire said they all could stay in the purple mansion
while they were in Chicago.

"Are you sure it's okay?" Jack wondered.

Yes, Claire was sure:

"I've written to my cousin Felicia,
telling her all about following Jesus,
and asking *What would Jesus do?*
Felicia says that's a perfect question,
and her parents think so too.
I'll write another letter today,
to tell her we're coming.
She'll be so glad to meet all of you!"

Later that night—in the moonlight—
in Mister Manning's house on Riddle Hill,
he and Jack prayed together
for God to keep them all safe in Chicago.

2

TWO RICH GIRLS

On a wide street
in the big city of Chicago
stood a handsome new house—
painted purple, with pink trim.
Next door was a bigger new house—
painted green, and trimmed in buttery yellow.

Almost every day, two girls played together
in front of these mansions—

Felicia Starr, who lived in the purple one,
and Penny Rose Ripple, who lived in the green one.

Penny Rose liked to talk about money and being rich.
One day she asked Felicia,
"Did you know my father owns more houses and
buildings than anyone else in Chicago?
He owns almost the entire Southside."

But Felicia didn't answer.
She liked to talk about making clothes,
because her mother was teaching her to sew.
With her mother's help,
Felicia had made a little blue blanket
for her dog, Little Dipper.

Penny Rose said to her,
"Oh, Felicia, you're so *strange!* Only poor girls sew."

While trying to wrap Little Dipper in the blanket,
Felicia answered, "Then being a poor girl
can't be all bad, because sewing is fun."

"Felicia, you mustn't talk like that!
Being poor is dreadful!"

"How do you know?"

"Because Father told me. Poor people live in all those houses he owns on the Southside. And he says those people are dirty and mean and horrible."

Just then, they heard two horses clip-clopping down the wide street, pulling a fancy coach. The driver stopped in front of the green house.

Out of the coach stepped Mister Ripple,
smoking a cigar.

Penny Rose ran to greet him.
"Hello, Father. I was just telling Felicia
about all the houses you own on the Southside."

Mister Ripple smiled
and made a little rumble in his throat
as he patted Penny Rose on the head.

Then Felicia had a question:
"Mister Ripple, sir,
are all your houses on the Southside
as big and pretty as this one?"

Mister Ripple answered in a grumbly voice,
without taking the cigar out of his mouth:
"What's that?
Oh — no, of course not!"

Then he rumbled a little more in his throat,
gave Felicia a pat on the head,
and hurried into the house.

3

UNHAPPY NEWS

As Felicia gave Little Dipper
a ride on the porch swing,
Penny Rose frowned at her friend.
"Felicia, that was a silly question to ask Father!
Don't you know that poor people
never live in mansions?"

Felicia kept swinging
while Penny Rose kept talking:
"Felicia, you're a rich girl!
Hasn't your father told you
that you must learn to think and talk
and behave like one?"

Felicia refolded the dog's blanket
while she answered:

"Not really. But once I got a letter
from my cousin Claire in the country.
She said she and all her friends were learning
to ask the question *What would Jesus do?*
So I asked Daddy about it, and he said
it's a perfect way to decide what's right
to think or say or do."

"Oh, that's crazy, Felicia.
You must have misunderstood what he said.
Why don't you ask your father
what it really means to be a rich girl?"

A few moments later in the purple house, Felicia
found her father at his desk in an upstairs room.

He was staring at a piece of paper.
Quickly she asked, "Daddy, am I a rich girl?"

Slowly he dropped the paper
and pulled Felicia into his arms.
In a sad, whispery voice he said,
"You were—but no longer, my darling daughter!
We're going to lose everything.
Everything!"

Then he dropped his face into his hands,
and said no more.

4

ON THE L&R RAILROAD

The day finally came
when Bill and Claire
and Jack and Mister Manning
gathered at the station
for the trip to Chicago.

But on that Thursday morning,
Bill was worried.
"Trains can have bad wrecks, can't they?"
Bill asked his friends.

Trains can, of course.
But Jack said something better to Bill
as they stepped on board:
"Remember the song we're learning in Sunday school
— the one about God's hands?

> *"He's got the whole world—in His hands,*
> *He's got the whole wide world—in His hands…*

"That means *everything*, Bill—
even the L & R Railroad.
Nothing will happen to it
unless God lets it happen. And He knows what's best."

By the time the train was chug-chugging toward
Chicago, they were all singing along…

"He's got the L & R Railroad—in His hands,
He's got the L & R Railroad—in His hands,

He's got the L & R Railroad—in His hands,
He's got the whole world in His hands!"

A few hours later,
the train slowed as it entered Chicago.
Mister Manning knew his friends were looking
out the window, and he said,
"Tell me what you see."

Jack answered,
"So many buildings and streets and horses
and wagons and carriages and people—
and more people, and *more* people, and *more!*
I wonder what they're like?"

"Like you and me," Mister Manning answered,
"except in one very important way:
So many of them here don't know about Jesus.
They don't know how much He loves them,
and they don't know how to follow Him."
When they were all off the train,
Mister Manning pulled the children closer and said,

"That's why I've come back.
While you're staying at the purple mansion,
I'll be walking the Chicago streets that I've known
for so many years, and and I'll pray to God
for the people of this city. That's my work here.
And I wonder what special jobs God has here
for you…"

5

FAST
TROUBLE

Outside the train station,
the children found a cab-carriage.

Mister Manning told the driver the address
of Claire's cousin. After paying money to the driver,
Mister Manning turned to the children.

"Claire, remember to ask Felicia's parents
to bring you back to the station
by ten o'clock Saturday morning.
And Bill—do you have our return tickets?"

"Yes, sir, all four—deep in my pocket,
with my silver dollar."

"Good. Keep those tickets tucked away
until we meet here again on Saturday.
We'll need them to get home.

"And don't take out your dollar
until you know it's time to spend it."

Bill agreed, then Mister Manning said goodbye
to the children. With only his cane to guide him,
he walked away, praying already
for the people of Chicago.
Soon he disappeared into the crowd.

As the cab-driver took up the reins of the horses,
he greeted his passengers and said,
"Did you hear about the new contest
the railroad is having?
If a blue star is printed on your ticket,
you get to choose a free train ride
to *anywhere* the railroad goes!"

Jack let out a whistle and said to Bill,
"We should check our tickets!"

Bill scratched his forehead.
"Mister Manning said to keep them tucked away
until Saturday. But I suppose he'd be glad
if we won another free trip.
He could go with us and pray for another city.
Okay, let's check."

With the station crowd pressing in
all around the carriage,
Bill pulled out the tickets
and held them in the daylight.
And quicker than you can say *creeper sweeper,*
an arm reached out from the crowd
and snatched those tickets from Bill's hands.

"HEY!"
Bill
cried
out.

But it was too late to catch the thief,
who had vanished into the crowd.
Bill moaned:
"I didn't even have time to check for blue stars!"

The driver said he was terribly sorry.
There was nothing the children could do
except ride on to the purple mansion
and meet Claire's cousin and her family.

On the way, the question *What would Jesus do?*
went through each of their minds.
Claire saw Bill's sad face and tried to cheer him up.
"Don't worry, Bill. It wasn't your fault.
Besides, Felicia and her parents
will help us buy new tickets."

"Thank you, Claire. But it *was* my fault.
I should have kept the tickets in my pocket,
like Mister Manning told me. I'm sorry."

Jack put his arm on Bill's shoulder.
"It was partly my fault too.
I asked you to check the tickets,
even though I knew what Mister Manning told you.
I'm sorry, too."

6

A CLOSED
DOOR

"We're nearly there.
Only one block to go!"
said the cab-driver.

The children decided to walk the rest of the way.
By arriving more quietly at the purple mansion,
they wanted to surprise Felicia.
The driver said goodbye and good luck,
then drove away.

But as the children neared the house,
they stopped and stared.

The front door was boarded up,
and all the windows were shuttered!

Then the children heard a voice above them:
"Looking for someone?"

They glanced up…and saw a girl
in an upstairs window next door—

in a
green
house,
with trim
as yellow
as butter.

Claire answered, "Yes.
We're here to visit Felicia Starr and her parents.
What happened? Where are they?"

The girl leaned further out the window.
"They can't live there anymore because they're poor.
I suppose they're staying in one of the
houses my father owns on the Southside.
He owns hundreds of them, you know."

Claire spoke louder now. "No, they aren't poor!
Felicia's father has *lots* of money!"

The girl in the window shook her head.
"Not anymore. My father says Mister Starr lost it all
in 'reckless speckle-ation,' whatever that means.
Oh, I hear Father calling me now."

She drew back inside and shut the window.

Meanwhile,
Jack had climbed the front steps of the purple house
and spotted a letter in the open mailbox
on the front porch.
"Look, Claire! There's your letter to Felicia.
Maybe she never even saw it."

It was true. Claire stared at the unopened letter.
"Oh, what do we do now?"
She looked at Jack, and Jack looked at Bill.

Then Bill looked up and prayed aloud:
"Lord Jesus, please help us.
We don't know where to go or what to do."

7

TO THE
SOUTHSIDE

As the children
turned back to the street,
Claire said,
"Where did that girl
say Felicia might be staying?"

Jack remembered, and looked to his left.
"She called it 'the Southside.'
And south is this way. Let's start walking
and I'm sure we'll find it."

So, southward they walked…
and walked…
and walked…

In time
they came to houses and buildings that were grimy
and shabby and jammed together,
with no front yards or flowers
or fences.

From a dark doorway, a boy stared out at them.
Jack gave him a smile and said,
"Can you tell me if this is the Southside?"
The boy laughed. "Ha! The Southside…
where you can't hide—outside…or inside!"
Laughing more, he stepped back into the darkness.

"What in the world does that mean?"
Bill asked.
As they kept walking,
Jack looked carefully around him and said,
"Maybe it means we're here."

The streets now were noisy and hot and smelly.
As the children stopped at a crowded corner,
Claire said, "I'm hungry and thirsty."

Bill reached into his pocket. "Don't forget: I still have
my silver dollar. It could buy our dinner."

Jack shook his head.
"No, I think you should save it.
It's all the money we've got,
and we have to buy new train tickets."

Bill fingered the smooth, round silver dollar
in his pocket.

Turning away from Jack and Claire,
he quietly pulled out the little treasure
just to see it shine.

And before you could say *jabber grabber*,
someone from the crowd pushed into him
and tripped him.

As Bill tumbled to the street,
he saw the silver dollar fly from his hand—
and into the fingers of the person who pushed him.
It looked like a boy—
but his hat was pulled so low over his head
that Bill couldn't see his face.

Bill yelled: "Stop him! Stop him!"
But the boy was gone,
and besides, no one in the noisy crowd
paid any attention to Bill.

Jack helped him to his feet.
"Bill, what happened?"

With a guilty groan,
Bill told his friends everything, and added,
"So we have no train tickets home,
no place to stay, no food—
and now no money. Ohhhhh!"

"But we're still in God's hands!"
Claire responded hopefully.

Beside the doorway to a nearby shop,
she sat down to rest her tired feet.
She quietly prayed: "Lord Jesus,
please don't forget us…"

8

A BIG MISTAKE

At the edge of the street,
Jack and Bill heard a commotion.
They saw people stepping aside
for a fancy coach that was fast approaching.
It was shiny green with bright yellow trim
and looked out of place here
among the ragged crowds
and run-down buildings.

"Out of the way, out of the way!" the coach driver called.

He pulled the horses to a stop
at the corner where the children were.
Down from the coach stepped a big man.
He was frowning and smoking a cigar.
While the coach waited,
the man marched into the doorway beside Claire,
and called out in a grumbly voice,
"Mickey Mallory, hand over that rent money at once!"

Suddenly Jack tapped Bill's shoulder. "Look!"

A boy was sneaking
under the fancy coach,
and crawling up to the seat—
where a fine fur coat
was lying.

The boy grabbed the coat. And almost before you could say *scratcher snatcher,* three things happened.

First,
as the boy jumped down from the seat,
his foot caught on the sideboard
and he fell into the street.

Second,
they all heard the grumbly voice
of the cigar-smoking man
as he came out the doorway.

Third,
when the boy with the fur coat saw the man,
he panicked. He threw the coat
onto Bill and Jack,
and ran away.

Bill and Jack each felt the grumbly man's fat fingers clawing deep into their shoulders.

"Now I've got you!" the man snarled,
blowing cigar smoke into the boys' faces.
The coach driver rushed down and grabbed both boys,
while the man with the cigar took back his fur coat.

"Take these robbers where they belong," he ordered.
Jack protested: "But sir, you're mistaken!
We didn't steal it."

With another growl, the man turned away.
Meanwhile the driver twisted their ears
and gave the boys a shove.
"You heard what Mister Ripple said!
Start walking, you rascals!"

Bill and Jack looked fearfully at each other.
Bill prayed:
"O Lord, help us do now what Jesus would do!"

"Quiet! Keep moving!" the driver shouted,
giving Bill a kick.

Claire watched with horror.
She cried out, "Stop! Wait! *No!*"

But the driver marched the boys away,
and they disappeared
from her sight.

9

A WELCOME FACE

"Oh, Lord,
I don't understand!"
Claire said,
as she wandered along.

Looking out through her tears,
Claire wished she could see the face of a friend.
But all she saw were dingy buildings,
and dirty streets,
and so many people in a noisy hurry.

She remembered what Mister Manning had said
about these people—
that so many of them didn't know Jesus.
But she *did* know Him.
Jesus was her Friend.

As the afternoon sky began to darken into evening,
Claire prayed again:
"Lord Jesus, please help me…"

Claire wanted to worry.
But instead she decided that singing would help…

"He's got the big, wide city—in His hands,
  He's got the big, lonely city—in His hands..."

Now she could almost feel an angel's arm around her.
She sang a little louder:

"He's got the hurry-scurry city—in His hands,
  He's got the whole world in His hands."

Claire heard someone else singing.
Could it be an angel's voice?

"He's got the whole world—in His hands..."

Standing on tiptoes, Claire looked ahead
through the crowd.
There on the next street corner,
behind a cart piled with cloth—

...was Felicia! Claire ran to meet her.

Little Dipper gave a happy bark
as Felicia hugged her cousin.
"Why, it *is* you, Claire!
Whatever are you doing here?"

In her excitement,
Claire tried to say everything at once:

"You didn't get my letter.
And your house is all shut up!
And someone stole our tickets and our money.
And my friends did nothing wrong,
but they were taken away and I don't know where!
And I've never had so much trouble in my life.
But I've been praying for help,
and I'm so glad to see you, Felicia!
But what are YOU doing here?"

Felicia lifted up a good-sized blanket
made from scrap-cloth.
"I made these myself. And I'm selling them—
but let me hear your story first.
I'm so glad you're here,
and you can stay with me tonight!"

Claire smiled, not so much at Felicia, but to God.
With a whisper of relief she prayed,
"Thank you, Lord!"

Then, with sadness, Claire told her cousin
about Jack and Bill and Mister Manning,
and how much she missed them.

10

A NEW FRIEND

Claire helped Felicia hold up
the blankets and towels
so people passing by
might see them and buy one.

Meanwhile,
Felicia told *her* story.

"Mother taught me how to sew these.
Selling them is our only way to make money
for our food and rent.
We live in a one-room apartment,
just Mother and me.
And Mother isn't well, Claire.
She's in bed all day because she's heartbroken.

"You see, something happened,
and Daddy had to pay someone all his money.
But our neighbor, Mister Ripple,
said it wasn't enough.
So Mister Ripple made us leave our home.
They put Daddy in jail
and they hardly ever let us visit him.
But the jailhouse has windows.
I go there every morning, and at eight o'clock
Daddy looks outside through the bars
and smiles at me and waves.
Tomorrow you can go too, Claire!
He'll be so happy to see you with me."

The girls heard a voice behind them saying,
"Felicia, who's your friend?"

They turned to see a boy
carrying a tray of wood carvings.

Felicia smiled at him.

"Hello, Stephen. This is my cousin Claire.

And Claire, this is Stephen Clyde.

He lives next door to Mother and me.

His father is a carpenter who's away looking for work.

He taught Stephen how to carve these things

from wood, and Stephen sells them."

On Stephen's tray

Claire saw tiny wooden furniture,

and crosses, and little wooden hands folded in prayer.

Stephen proudly showed each one to Claire,
then said to her,
"Has Felicia told you about the *Big Plan?*"

When Claire said no, Stephen explained.
"We thought of it all by ourselves,
just by asking the question *What would Jesus do?*
We have lots of time to talk about it,
because I meet Felicia here each evening
to walk her home."

"These streets can be dangerous,"
Felicia said, looking all around them.
"Especially now. The Stealer Gang
has been robbing nearly everyone."

Stephen put his carvings on top
of Felicia's scrap-blankets.
As he began pushing the cart home for her,
he asked, "By the way, Felicia,
how much did you make today?"

"Fifty cents—for one blanket.
How about you, Stephen?"

Stephen smiled. "It was my best day yet.
I made ninety-five cents—nearly a dollar!"

Just then Little Dipper barked at an alley-kitten
that was dodging the fast-moving legs and wheels
on the street.

Felicia saw it too.
"Look! Dipper's found a poor kitty.
Claire, let's catch it and take it home and feed it.
We'll be right back, Stephen."

11

THE STEALER
GANG

The girls
followed the kitten
into a dark alley.

"Here, kittee, kittee, kit-teeeee,"
Felicia called in the darkness,
with Claire right behind her.

Suddenly,
hands reached out and grabbed them.
Little Dipper barked,
and the girls screamed: "Help! Help!"

Stephen was quickly there,
but someone grabbed him too.

When a lamp was lit, they saw themselves
surrounded by boys armed with heavy sticks.

"The Stealer Gang!" said Stephen,
and two boys tightened their grip on his arms.

"Keep quiet—and put up your hands,"
ordered the gang leader, who held the lamp.
Stephen nodded to Claire and Felicia,
and they held their arms high.
The leader smiled. "Yes, we're the Stealer Gang,
and we've been watching you. It's been a good day
for making money, hasn't it? You've made yours…
now we'll make ours.
I figure we'll get about a dollar and a half from you.

"So hand over your money to my partner, Burnsy."
A boy carrying a burlap bag stepped up
to the children. Stephen whispered to Felicia,
"Don't be afraid." They lowered their arms and took
from their pockets all they had earned that day.
They dropped the coins into Burnsy's bag, then raised
their arms again. Burnsy stepped up to Claire and
said, "*Your* money, too!"

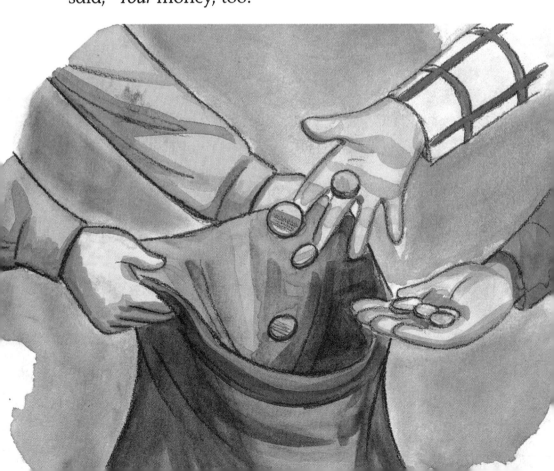

Claire shook her head.
"I haven't any. But money won't help you, anyway.
An old blind man named Mister Manning
knows what you really need,
and he's praying that you'll find it."

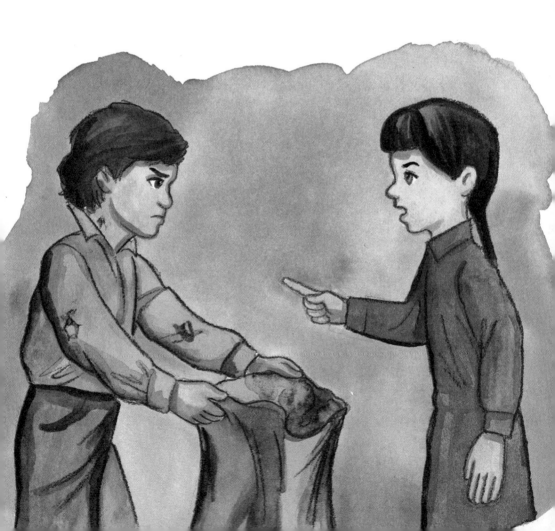

Behind Burnsy,
the gang leader suddenly raised the lamp higher
for a better look at Claire, and he said,
"Mister Manning? *Old blind Mister Manning?*
You know him?"

Claire answered bravely again:
"He's my friend. And right now
he's walking the streets of this city,
praying for people like you.
He and I came on a train today
with two other friends. But now we're all apart,
and our money and train tickets have been stolen—
probably by your gang here.
But we're in God's hands.
He knows all about *us,* and all about *you!*"

The gang leader looked sadly at the money bag,
then again at the three children.

And what he said next
took everyone by surprise.

12

JASPER CHASE

"You can put down your hands,"
the gang leader said
to Stephen and the girls.
"I'm giving back your money."

With alarm, Burnsy turned on his leader.
"Giving it *back?* Are you crazy?"

"Maybe I have been," the leader said,
still looking at the children.
"I met Mister Manning a year ago.
He told me about Jesus, and it sounded right
and good. That old blind man prayed with me,
and I told him I believed in Jesus
and would always try to follow Him.
But I guess I've been following the devil instead."

Stephen calmly stepped forward and asked, "What's your name?"

"Jasper...Jasper Chase."
Then Stephen said quietly,
"Jasper, the devil wants you,
but he can never steal you from God's hands.
God is stronger than the devil, and He'll protect you,
if you really want to follow God—
if you really want to *stay* in His hands..."
Stephen saw a look of hope on Jasper's face,
and he continued speaking:
"Tomorrow night we're having a gospel meeting
in the empty warehouse across the street,
and we'll talk about this more.
Please come—all of you. Will you?"

Burnsy gripped his leader's shoulder.
"Jasper, don't listen to him! Let's get out of here!"

Jasper faced his partner and said quietly,
"Burnsy, return their money like I told you to."
With an ugly glare,
Burnsy reached into the burlap bag
and pulled out Stephen and Felicia's money.

Giving it back, he said to them,

"Yeah, maybe we'll be at your gospel meeting.
But if we are, you'll be sorry!
We know how to make trouble.
Let's get out of here, guys!" With that,
Burnsy and all the Stealers
quickly slipped away.

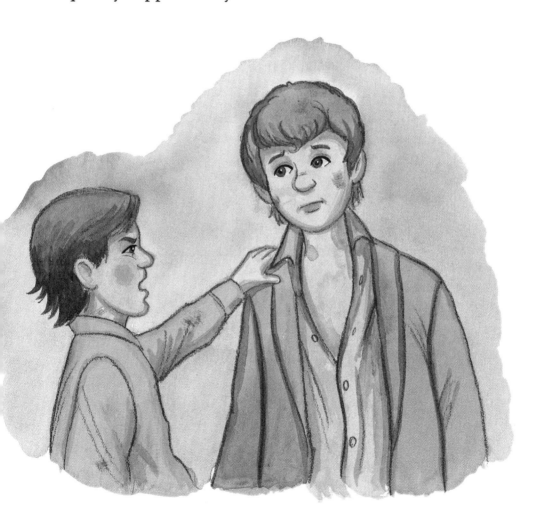

All, that is, except Jasper.
He turned to the children.
"I'll try to come tomorrow night—
and not to make trouble. But first there's someone
I need to find—and soon! Good night!"

Then Jasper, too,
disappeared into the darkness.

13

IN JAIL

In the Southside Jailhouse
that night it was just as dark inside
as outside. And inside was where
Bill and Jack were—
locked away in a cell.

They were lying on the bare floor,
staring at the ceiling. After a stretch of silence,
Bill asked, "Jack, was Jesus ever in jail?"

Before he could answer, Jack heard a noise.
He slipped off his shoe and threw it at a rat
in the corner of the cell. Then he laid back down
and said, "I don't think so, Bill.
But Paul was locked up lots of times.
Do you remember the story of when he and Silas
sang to the Lord one night in jail?"
Jack began singing:

 I have decided to follow Jesus…

Bill joined in:

 We have decided to follow Jesus…

"Stop your awful racket!" came a cranky voice
from another cell. "No, please *don't* stop!"
said someone else. It was the prisoner in the cell next
to Jack and Bill. Though the boys didn't know it,
the man was Mister Starr, Felicia's father.

He said to them, "That song reminds me of my darling daughter. I'll sing it with you."

So the man and the boys filled their corner of the jailhouse with that beautiful song.

Then Mister Starr said, "Why are you boys here?"

Jack and Bill told him what had happened to them,
because of the cigar-smoking man
in the fancy green-and-yellow coach.

Mister Starr sighed.
"Ah, yes. That would be Mister Ripple.
All these men in jail are here because of him—
because they owe him money.
And he won't let them work to pay him back."

Bill pressed his face to the bars of their cell.
"Sir, is Mister Ripple the reason *you're* here too?"

Mister Starr replied,
"Yes, and in more ways than one, I believe.
Mister Ripple is one of the most powerful men
in Chicago, and once he was my next-door neighbor.
He doesn't know Jesus, and I fear
I didn't pray for him enough back then.
But now I have plenty of time to pray for him—
and plenty of reason, too.
After all, Jesus tells us to pray even for our enemies."

Now Jack was standing with Bill
beside the bars of their cell, and he said…

"Sir, would you like us to pray with you now
for Mister Ripple?" So together, in the darkness
of the Southside Jailhouse, the boys and Mister Starr
prayed for the man who put them there.
Not far away at that moment,

someone else was praying in the darkness.
But of course, to the blind Mister Manning
night was just as bright as daytime.
His light was inside him, so he knew no darkness.
From the houses along the street where Mister
Manning walked, he could hear children crying
and mothers and fathers yelling. He talked with God
about each person
he heard.

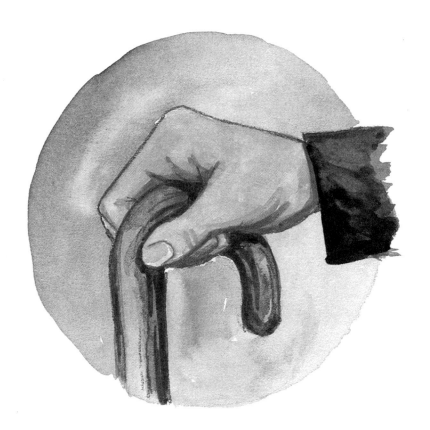

"O Lord, my Father and my Friend,
these people and this city are in Your hands.
Please show me how I can help someone here..."

14

ASTONISHING PLANS

In a shoddy one-room home that night,
a group of friends were sharing
a simple dinner.

There was buttermilk and leftover breakfast biscuits
and turnip stew. Stephen Clyde was there with Felicia
and Claire, plus Little Dipper and the alley-kitten.
Mrs. Starr was in her bed in the corner.
While cleaning the dishes together,
Claire asked Stephen to tell her more
about the gospel meeting he had mentioned
to Jasper Chase.

Stephen replied, "That's the *Big Plan*
Felicia and I have been working on.
First, we decided on the warehouse.
We needed a big place,
because we want lots of people there. You see,
so many Southside men go to the saloons at night
and waste their money getting drunk.
The women at home with the children
can only worry and cry.
We want to give them something better to do:
a gospel meeting, where we can tell everyone
about the Lord Jesus."

"*Who* will tell them?" Claire asked.

Stephen grinned. "Well, if no one else will, *I* will."

"So will I," said Felicia, as she unfolded
a scrap-cloth banner with four special words upon it :
WHAT WOULD JESUS DO?
"I made it to hang in the warehouse,
which tomorrow night we'll call the *Sharehouse*.

"We'll share the good news about Jesus,
and we'll also share a wonderful hot meal
with everyone there."

Claire wondered where all the food would come from,
and who would cook it.
Felicia and Stephen looked at each other.
Stephen finally answered, "We don't really know yet."

Claire had another question:
"Do you have permission from the owner
of the warehouse—the *Sharehouse,* that is—
to use it tomorrow night?"
With the slightest droop in his shoulders,
Stephen replied, "No...not yet.
But we plan to visit him in the morning
and ask him."

Claire was astonished.
"There's still so much to be done—
you need more time.
Why must the meeting be tomorrow?"

This time Felicia answered: "Tomorrow's my birthday.
Daddy's in jail, and Mother is sick,
so they won't be able to celebrate with me…

But having a big gospel meeting on the Southside
will be a miracle! It will make this birthday my best ever."

Stephen took an old coffee tin
down from a shelf
and showed Claire
several coins
stored inside.

"We're doing all we can for the meeting.
We've saved this money to help buy the food.
I know it isn't enough.
But on our own we'll *never* have enough.
We know this gospel meeting is in God's hands.
Only He can make it happen."

Stephen looked closer into the face of his new friend.
"Will you help us, Claire? Will you pray with us,
and go with us tomorrow
when we talk to the warehouse owner?"

The four special words went through Claire's mind.
Then she joined hands with Stephen and Felicia
and said, "Yes! Let's pray for a miracle!"

15

A MIDNIGHT
MEETING

It was nearly midnight
when Jasper finally found
the person he was seeking.

He didn't want to startle the man,
so he called out to him across the darkness:
"Mister Manning— do you remember
the boy Jasper Chase?"

Hearing the voice,
Mister Manning stopped his pacing and praying.
"Jasper? Jasper, is that you?
I've been talking with God about you this very night."

"So you *do* remember!" Jasper said…

as the two of them met in the middle of the empty street.

Mister Manning remembered more: "In these streets
I met a boy in trouble, and I told him about the only
One whose hands could save him from that trouble.
That boy was you, Jasper. And you promised
you would follow Jesus.
Jasper, have you kept
your promise?"

In sorrow Jasper admitted, "No, not even for a week."
He told all about his part in the Stealer Gang,
then said, "Tonight I heard a brave girl say
that you were back in the city,
praying for all of us here.
Mister Manning, is it too late for me to follow Jesus?
Have I been too wicked?
Have I stolen too much money?"

Quickly and silently,
Mister Manning prayed again for this boy.

Then he answered, "No, Jasper, it isn't too late.
God made you with His own hands,
and you're worth a billion times more
than all the money you could ever steal.
No, it isn't too late. God is good,
and He's given you more time.
So be strong! You need never go back
to the Stealer Gang again.
Come walk with me and let's talk about it."

Jasper felt stronger already
as Mister Manning added, "And please
tell me more about the brave girl you mentioned."

16

BIRTHDAY MORNING

The next morning
was beautiful
and bright.

Felicia gave her mother breakfast
and a goodbye kiss.

Then she and Claire and Stephen Clyde
walked to the Southside Jailhouse.
They stood below a certain window, and waited.

At eight o'clock,
through the thick glass and heavy bars,
they saw the face of Felicia's father appear.

He smiled to see Felicia's friends standing with her.

As Felicia waved to him,
she saw his lips form the words,
"Happy Birthday, Darling!"
He blew her a kiss,
then stepped back out of sight.

Quietly,
with Little Dipper at their heels,
the children walked on.

Then Stephen pointed out a building
that looked to Claire like a big barn.
"That's the Southside Warehouse.
It's empty now; the owner plans to tear it down soon
to build a bigger one.
His name is Mister Ripple.
Felicia says he lives in a green mansion
nextdoor to where she used to live."

Claire remembered that house,
and where it was.
She knew they had a long walk ahead of them,
and none of them could say
what might happen when they got there.

But the morning sun was pouring out
golden gladness from God's hands,
and the children were happy to have Him
as their Father.

17

A CHANGED MAN

Hot and tired,
the children finally reached
the Ripple mansion.
At the door they met
a very worried Penny Rose.

"I'm glad you've come to see Father.
He had a frightful dream last night,
and that's all he'll talk about.
Now he says he's waiting for an angel.
It's so *strange.*
He hasn't listened to any of us—
but maybe you can help him."

Upstairs in his bedroom, Mister Ripple
was still in his nightshirt and barefooted.
His hair was rumpled,
and for once he had no cigar.

He was pacing back and forth across the carpeted floor.

When he caught sight of the children
at the bedroom door, he gulped his breath.
Gripping a bedpost with both hands,
he said to his visitors,
"Are you from heaven?"

Felicia responded nervously,
"Sir, remember me?
I'm Felicia Starr, Penny Rose's friend.
I used to live next door to you,
and you used to pat my head.
And this is my cousin Claire
and my friend Stephen Clyde."

Mister Ripple stared at them.

Then Stephen said politely, "If you please, sir,
we've come to ask you to *do* something— *now.*"

Suddenly Mister Ripple's face burst into a smile.

He flung his arms in the air and shouted,
"*All morning* I've been asking God to send someone
to tell me *exactly what to do next.*
So *you* are the answer to my prayer!"

In a hurry, Mister Ripple began
putting on his clothes over his nightshirt.

"You see, children,
last night in a dream
I'm sure I saw the Judgment Day—
and the Lord Himself.
I said to Him, 'O Lord, I believe in You now!'

"Then I saw just His finger—
pointing at *me!*—
and He said,
'What about the men and boys you threw in prison?
What about the people who pay too much
to live in those wretched houses you own—
where they sweat in summer and freeze in winter?
What about the saloons you own,
where men waste their *money* and their *time,*
two good gifts that come from My hand?'

"I answered at once,
'What should I do, Lord? What would YOU do?'

And then…*the vision faded away!*
But I knew God would send someone
to answer my questions."

Pulling on a pair of boots
over his bare feet, he asked the children,
"So, what is it you want me to do?"

18

THE
SHAREHOUSE

In his fancy coach,
Mister Ripple and the children
rode at once to the Southside Jailhouse.
Mister Ripple wanted to set free not only Mister Starr,
but everyone in the jail. What a surprise it was
for Claire to see Jack and Bill walk out
with all the others!

They all went next to the warehouse to prepare for the gospel meeting. Mister Ripple ordered mountains of food,

and an army of cooks and waiters,
and wagonloads of flowers
and decorations.

ide
OUSE
TONIGHT!

KERY

227

That night,
Felicia's mother and father
came with her to the gospel meeting,
where they celebrated her best birthday ever.

Mister Manning appeared
with Jasper, and was together again
with Jack and Bill and Claire.

Penny Rose was there with her father.
She was still trying to understand
what had happened to him,
especially when he stood to make
this announcement to everyone:

"I'm going to do what Jesus would do.
Instead of building a new warehouse,
I promise to rebuild all the shabby houses I own
on the Southside.
I'm also shutting down all the saloons I own,
to encourage you men to stay
with your families at night."

But when Stephen Clyde stood up to speak,
Burnsy and the Stealer Gang
stepped out from the crowd
and began throwing rocks and rotten eggs at him.

The other people quickly stopped them,
and Mister Ripple rose and called out
to the boys,

"The Southside will be a new place,
and you can live here in a new way.
Listen now to this boy Stephen Clyde,
and he'll tell you how to have a good life forever."

And that's exactly what Stephen told them all.
Then he held up a wooden cross he had carved
and said, "Jesus died for all of us,
to take away the wrong things we've done.
And now He's alive, to be your Friend forever,
and to hold you in His hands if you'll ask Him.
You can be God's children
and someday live in His mansion in heaven!"

Hearing Stephen speak, many people cried
as they remembered the evil things they had done.
They said, "Please pray with us!"
So Mister Manning and the children did.

Along with those tears,
there was more food and music
and laughter and true joy at that meeting
than had ever been known in Chicago.

And the whole crowd sang,

"He's got the Southside Sharehouse—in His hands,
He's got the Southside Sharehouse—in His hands..."

As they were singing,
two of the Stealer boys reached for Bill's hand.
In it they placed a silver dollar, and four train tickets.

Bill thanked the boys,
and dropped the dollar in his pocket.
Then he and Jack glanced at the tickets.

Yes—they saw a blue star!

Immediately they both wondered
where in the world they might go next!

And tucking away the tickets,
they sang out with their friends...

*"He's got the whole world
in His hands!"*

QUESTIONS
TO TALK ABOUT
TOGETHER

Chapter 1—Winning Big

- How much money did Bill win?
- What different things did Bill want to do with the money he won?
- If *you* were Bill, what would you have done with the money?
- Who were Bill's best friends?

Chapter 2—Two Rich Girls

- What do Penny Rose and Felicia like to talk about?
- What do *you* like to talk about?
- Who is teaching Felicia to sew?
- Is Penny Rose thinking the right way about poor people?
- What does Jesus think about poor people?

Chapter 3—Unhappy News

- What is the name of Felicia's dog?
- Felicia knows about the question *What would Jesus do?* How did she learn about this question?
- When does asking *What would Jesus do?* help you to decide what is right to think or say or do?

Chapter 4—On the L&R Railroad

- Why was Bill worried?
- The children sang a song about Someone who had the whole world in His hands. Who is this Person?
- When their train arrived in Chicago, what did the children see when they looked out the window?
- What is Mister Manning going to do while he is in Chicago? And why is he going to do this?
- What special jobs do you think God might have for the children to do while they are in Chicago?

Chapter 5—Fast Trouble

- What did Mister Manning ask Bill to do with the train tickets?
- Why did Bill take the tickets out of his pocket?
- While the children rode in the cab-carriage on their way to the purple mansion, what were they thinking about?
- Now that their train tickets are gone, how do you think the children will get back to their homes in the country?

Chapter 6—A Closed Door

- When the carriage was almost at the purple mansion, why did the children decide to walk the rest of the way?
- Who is the girl in the upstairs window?
- What did Bill pray?
- What do you think the children should do now?

Chapter 7—To the Southside

- Why are the children going to the Southside?
- The children were tired and hungry and thirsty. When was the last time you were tired and hungry and thirsty?
- Why doesn't Bill have his silver dollar anymore?
- What do you think will happen to the children next?

Chapter 8—A Big Mistake

- Who is the big man riding in the fancy green coach?
- Jack and Bill saw a boy sneaking under the fancy coach. What wrong things did this boy do?
- What did Bill pray?
- What do you think Claire should do now?

Chapter 9—A Welcome Face

- What did Claire remember about the people in the big city?
- Claire wanted to worry. But she decided to do something else. What was it?
- What do you do when you feel like worrying?
- When Felicia said that Claire could stay at her house tonight, what did Claire do?
- Claire is with her cousin Felicia now, but something is still making her sad. What is it?

Chapter 10—A New Friend

- Where is Felicia living now? And where are her mother and father?
- Where does the money come from to buy food for Felicia and her mother?
- What does Felicia do every morning at eight o'clock?
- What does Stephen Clyde make when he carves wood?
- Who taught Stephen to carve wood?
- What do you think will happen next?

Chapter 11—The Stealer Gang

- What are the boys in the Stealer Gang like?
- How does the Stealer Gang know how much money Stephen and Felicia have made today?
- Claire said that Mister Manning knew what the Stealer Gang really needs. What do you think it is?
- What do you think the leader of the Stealer Gang will say next?
- Are Claire and Stephen and Felicia still in God's hands?

Chapter 12—Jasper Chase

- Jasper remembers what Mister Manning told him a year ago. What did Mister Manning tell him?
- Stephen talked with Jasper about staying in God's hands. Can the devil steal us from God's hands?
- What wrong things is Burnsy doing?
- Who do you think Jasper wants to go see tonight?

Chapter 13—In Jail

- Jack talked about the story of Paul and Silas, when they sang one night in jail. What do you know about this Bible story?
- Why does Mister Starr like the song that Jack and Bill were singing?
- Mister Starr remembered that Jesus tells us to pray for our enemies. Who are some enemies we can pray for?
- Are Jack and Bill still in God's hands?
- What does Mister Manning hear as he walks in the streets of the city?

Chapter 14—Astonishing Plans

- What did Stephen and Felicia and Claire have for dinner?
- What is the Big Plan that Stephen and Felicia tell Claire about?
- Why does Felicia want to have the gospel meeting tomorrow?
- What do you think Stephen and Felicia and Claire will pray now?

Chapter 15—A Midnight Meeting

- What does Mister Manning remember about the boy Jasper Chase?
- Why do you think Jasper did not keep his promise about following Jesus?
- Why is it not too late for Jasper to follow Jesus now?
- What do you think Jasper should do now?
- What does God like best—people, or money?

Chapter 16—Birthday Morning

- What two things did Felicia give her mother?
- Even though she couldn't hear the words, what did Felicia's father tell her when he looked out at her from the jailhouse window?
- What are the children happy about this morning?
- What has made you happy today?
- How is God protecting the children in this story?
- What is God teaching the children in this story?

Chapter 17—A Changed Man

- Why is Penny Rose worried?
- Why is Mister Ripple waiting for an angel?
- In Mister Ripple's dream, what questions did Jesus ask him?
- Who did God send to answer Mister Ripple's questions?

Chapter 18—The Sharehouse

- What did Mister Ripple do at the jailhouse?
- How did Mister Ripple help the children get ready for the gospel meeting?
- At the gospel meeting, what promises did Mister Ripple make to the people there?
- Why do you think Stephen held up a wooden cross when he was talking to the people?
- Why did some people cry after Stephen spoke?
- Where do you think the children might go next?
- What does God have in His hands?